SNOWMOBILE RACING

SNOWMOBILE RACING

NICOLE PULEO

Lerner Publications Company ■ Minneapolis, Minnesota

ACKNOWLEDGMENTS: The illustrations are reproduced through the courtesy of: pp. 4, 33, The United States Suzuki Motor Corporation; pp. 7, 9, 11, 13, 15, 17, 19, 21, 23, 27, 29, 37, 39, Karl Knutson; pp. 25, 31, 35, Arctic Enterprises, Incorporated.

LIBRARY OF CONGRESS CATALOGING IN PUBLICATION DATA

Puleo, Nicole.
  Snowmobile racing.

  (Superwheels and Thrill Sports)
  SUMMARY: Describes the techniques of snowmobile racing and the rules in the various categories of snowmobile competition.

  1. Snowmobiles—Juvenile literature. [1. Snowmobile racing] I. Title.

GV857.S6P84   796.9   72-5422
ISBN 0-8225-0402-2

International Standard Book Number: 0-8225-0402-2
Library of Congress Catalog Card Number: 72-5422

5 6 7 8 9 10 85 84 83 82 81 80 79

INTRODUCTION

Not so long ago, many people living in Canada and the northern United States stayed indoors whenever possible during the cold winter months. They passed the time by talking, playing games, listening to the radio, reading, or by sitting around a coal-burning stove. Of course, rugged outdoorsmen have always enjoyed winter sports—skating, skiing, tobogganing, ice fishing, sledding, and the unpopular "sport" of shoveling snow. But today, even people who prefer the indoors are leaving the warmth and comfort of their homes to participate in an exciting new winter sport—snowmobiling.

A snowmobile is a motorized sled weighing about 450 pounds. It is powered by a piston or rotary engine. The engine moves a wide rubber track, or belt, that grips the snow and propels the vehicle forward. The machine is directed by two steel skis that are attached to the front. Since the skis are steered by handlebars, riding a snowmobile is something like riding a bicycle. In a snowmobile, the lever on the left handlebar controls the brakes, while the throttle lever on the right handlebar controls the gas.

The first successfully marketed snowmobile was built by Joseph-Armand Bombardier of Quebec, Canada. Bombardier began working on snowmobiles in the early 1930s, shortly after the tragic death of one of his sons. Stricken with appendicitis, the boy had died because of a lack of medical attention; the roads of rural Quebec had been blocked with snow, making it impossible for Bombardier to get his son to a doctor. After the needless death of his son, Bombardier vowed to design a motorized sled that would cross the snow and prevent snow-caused tragedies like the one he had suffered.

In the late 1950s Bombardier perfected his machine, calling it a "snowmobile." At first, the machine was used mainly as a service vehicle by doctors, mailmen, and policemen in snow-clogged areas. But before long, the recreational value of the snowmobile was also discovered. In 1960, there were about 300 snowmobiles in the United States and Canada; by 1970, there were over a million.

Today, snowmobiling is the fastest growing winter sport in the world. It has become the new way to go places and to do things in the wintertime. And one of the things that snowmobilers enjoy doing the most is racing. Over 2,000 snowmobile clubs have been established in the United States and Canada, and nearly all of these clubs have racing programs. They also participate in trail rides, camping trips, "snowfaris," and other exciting snowmobile activities.

Each winter, more and more people take to snowmobile racing — one of the most fun-filled motor sports of all. By 1978, there were 3 million snowmobiles in the United States and Canada.

Several things explain the growing popularity of snowmobile racing: it's fun and exciting, it's easy to learn, and it's open to young and old alike. Most kinds of motor racing limit competition to adult men, but snowmobile racing is truly a family sport, in which everyone from age 12 on up can join. The openness of snowmobile racing explains why the sport claims more women drivers than any other type of motor racing.

One possible drawback to snowmobile racing is that it can be quite expensive. In comparison to a regular snowmobile, which costs about $2,000, a snowmobile that has been designed or modified for racing can cost $4,000 or more. Of course, a racing snowmobile has a more powerful engine and can travel at much greater speeds than an ordinary one. While a purely recreational snowmobile travels anywhere from 15 to 45 miles per hour (mph), a snowmobile racer can go over 100 mph. In 1972, Charles Lofton of Thief River Falls, Minnesota, set a record snowmobile speed mark of 139.8 mph.

Powerful engines enable some snowmobiles to race at speeds of over 100 mph.

SNOWMOBILE ASSOCIATIONS

Many snowmobile associations have been established in the United States and Canada for the specific purpose of sanctioning, or giving approval to, snowmobile races. Among these organizations are the Canadian Snowmobile Association, the Western Snowmobile Association, the American Snowmobile Association, and the United States Snowmobile Association.

THE UNITED STATES SNOWMOBILE ASSOCIATION

The oldest, largest, and most influential snowmobile organization in this country is the United States Snowmobile Association, or the USSA. Established in 1965 to set up the rules and class divisions for snowmobile racing, the organization has its headquarters in Rhinelander, Wisconsin. Each year, the USSA sanctions over 1,000 races in the United States and Canada.

All of the snowmobiles that compete in USSA races are labeled as "stock," "modified," or "non-production" machines. Both stock and modified snowmobiles start off as ordinary production models, or snowmobiles available to the general public for pleasure riding. The extent to which the snowmobiles are altered for racing is what determines whether they are stock or modified machines.

Oval-track racing is one of the USSA's most popular categories of snowmobile competition.

A stock snowmobile is one that has been altered only slightly for safety reasons. While cleats, padding, and improved brakes may be added to the machine, and while the windshield, headlights, and backrest may be removed, a stock snowmobile must have the original engine, track, and skis supplied by the manufacturer. A modified snowmobile, on the other hand, is one that has been greatly altered to improve its power and maneuverability as a racing machine; all of its original parts, including the engine, may be altered.

Differing from both stock and modified machines are non-production snowmobiles, which the USSA defines as "homemade, non-commercially built, or custom-made" snowmobiles of any size or shape. In spite of their differences, all three categories of snowmobiles share three things in common: they all must run on ordinary pump gasoline, they all must be equipped with mufflers, and they all must meet the safety requirements of the United States Snowmobile Association.

In the interest of fair competition, the USSA runs separate races for stock, modified, and non-production machines. The USSA further promotes fair competition by subdividing all three types of snowmobiles on the basis of engine size, which is measured in cubic centimeters. This prevents snowmobiles with powerful engines from racing against machines with less powerful engines.

This is a stock snowmobile, or one that has been altered only slightly.

By establishing five broad classes of snowmobile racing, the United States Snowmobile Association has given almost every snowmobile rider a chance to compete in the sport. All of the classes are based upon the age and sex of the riders and upon the designations and engine sizes of their machines. Boys and girls between 12 and 15 years old compete in the Junior Class, in which only stock snowmobiles are allowed. For men 16 years or older, there are two Senior classes—the Stock Class and the Modified Class. Women 16 years or older compete in the Women's Class. As in the Junior Class, only stock snowmobiles are allowed in this class. Finally, both men and women 16 years or older can race in the Non-Production Class, which is the most open class of all. As mentioned earlier, all USSA racing classes are further subdivided on the basis of engine size.

Whatever class they are racing in, all snowmobilers must follow the rules and regulations of the USSA. Rigidly enforced, these rules make snowmobile racing even safer than pleasure riding. (In fact, fewer accidents occur in supervised races than in any other type of snowmobile activity.) Above all, the United States Snowmobile Association requires that all snowmobiles be thoroughly examined for safety and alterations by a technical inspector before racing. If a machine fails to pass the inspection, or if it is using

The starting lineup of a well-attended race

any type of fuel other than ordinary pump gasoline, it is automatically disqualified from the race.

As for the drivers, they also are subject to strictly enforced rules. If a driver jumps the start of a race, or if he exhibits unsportsman-like behavior during a race (careless driving, blocking, crowding, or bumping), he can be disqualified from the race and suspended from racing for up to three years. A driver can also be disqualified for being under the influence of liquor or drugs, or for using vulgar and offensive language.

All the drivers who compete in USSA-sanctioned races are required to wear a lot of protective gear. This gear includes insulated fiberglass crash helmets, leather-lined face masks, shatterproof goggles, insulated boots that come up above the ankles, long gloves that come halfway up the elbows, and shin and knee guards. Most drivers also wear a one-piece suit that consists of a wind-resist-ant, water-repellent outer shell with a heavily insulated inner lining.

Helmets, goggles, and face masks are worn by all the drivers who compete in USSA races.

SPONSORS

All USSA races require sponsors. Sponsors enforce the USSA's rules, furnish the facilities for racing, and provide the personnel required to run a fair, safe race. The major sponsors of USSA races are snowmobile clubs and snowmobile manufacturers. When large manufacturers (Ski-Doo, Polaris, Arctic Cat, and others) sponsor snowmobile races, they usually enter their own factory teams. And in order to attract the best drivers and machines, manufacturers usually offer large cash prizes to the winners.

Any manufacturer or club sponsoring a USSA race must provide the personnel needed to run the race safely and fairly.

Among the most important officials at any snowmobile race are the paddock marshall, the chief starter, the corner men, and the chief scorer.

The paddock marshall is the man in charge of the warm-up and "paddock" areas. If a racer drives recklessly in the warm-up area— the place where drivers test their machines and "warm up" for the race—the paddock marshall can disqualify him from the race. The paddock marshall also controls everything that goes on in the paddock area, the place near the race track where all the competing drivers assemble with their machines just before the start of the race. He makes

Located near the race track is the paddock area, which serves as a parking lot for snowmobiles.

sure that only registered drivers are in this area and that no "funny business" (like someone tampering with another driver's machine) goes on. The paddock marshall also determines the starting lineup of the drivers in the race. His word is law, and he can disqualify any racer who doesn't cooperate with him or who fails to follow the rules of the United States Snowmobile Association.

The chief starter, as his name suggests, is the man who starts the race. Once the race is under way, he controls everything that happens on the racing track or course. If the chief starter feels it is necessary (because of an accident or bad weather), he can even stop the race. The chief starter is sometimes called the "flagman" because he uses flags to keep the race under control. A green flag means that "the race has been started" or that "the course is clear." While the yellow "caution" flag means, "slow down, hold your position, and do not pass," the blue flag with the yellow diagonal stripe is a "yield" flag meaning, "do not continue blocking the machine behind you." The red "danger" flag means that the race has been stopped, and the black flag—the one that racers never want to see—means that a racer has been disqualified for safety reasons or for misconduct. Finally, the white flag means that there is "one lap to go;" and the checkered flag (as in most kinds of racing), that the race is over.

Dropping the green flag, the chief starter signals the start of a race.

The corner men and the chief scorer are the other important officials at snowmobile races. The corner men assist the chief starter by using flags to control the action around the corners of the track or course, and the chief scorer determines and displays the final results of each race. In many cases, the chief scorer has an official timer working under him to clock the race.

Besides providing personnel, the people who sponsor snowmobile races must also furnish the facilities for racing. These facilities include warm-up and paddock areas, pit areas (areas off the track or course where drivers go when their machines are having mechanical difficulties), and safe race tracks and courses. In order to insure safety, sponsors often remove snow from the track or pack the snow down. Sponsors mark all the corners of a race track, and they use hazard markers to warn drivers of barbed wire and other hazards on obstacle and cross-country courses. To protect and control spectators, sponsors put up fencing between the track and the spectators.

Sponsors must also provide fire equipment, track equipment, and emergency equipment for snowmobile racing. The track equipment includes flag markers, fencing, a public address system, timing devices, snow-removing equipment, and at least two tow trucks. The emergency equipment includes at least two emergency vehicles, stretchers, and a good first-aid kit. Most sponsors also make sure that a doctor is in attendance in case of an accident or injury during the race.

Snowmobiles whiz around a flag-marked corner. If the blind corners of a race track were not marked, they could be very dangerous.

CATEGORIES OF SNOWMOBILE RACING

Although snowmobile racing is a relatively late arrival among winter sports, it offers almost as much variety as automobile racing. Six of the most important categories of snowmobile competition are road racing, oval-track racing, cross-country racing, slalom racing, hillclimbing, and drag racing.

ROAD RACING

One of the most popular types of snowmobile competition is road racing, which is also called "closed-course racing." In this kind of competition, snowmobilers race on a narrow road-like course that begins with a long straightaway, turns off into a hilly wooded area, and then returns to the straightaway where the race began. Wide enough to permit three snowmobiles to travel abreast, a road-racing course must be between two and three miles long. The number of laps around the course determines the total length of the race, and the first driver to cross the finish line after completing the specified number of laps is the winner.

Competing racers speed down the straightaway section of a road-racing course.

OVAL-TRACK RACING

Another popular category of snowmobile competition is oval-track racing. In this type of competition, snowmobilers race against each other on oval tracks enclosed with fencing. The tracks feature wide corners, long sections of straightaway, and a smooth running surface. Between one and two miles long and at least 50 feet wide, the entire layout of an oval snowmobile track is visible to the spectators. As in road racing, the number of laps around the track (usually 10) determines the total length of an oval-track race.

In oval-track racing, as in *all* types of snowmobile competition, separate races are held for each of the racing classes (Junior, Stock, Modified, and so on). If more than 12 machines from the same class show up for an oval-track race, short run-off races are usually held to cut the field down to 6 or 8 finalists.

After the finalists have been determined in the run-off events, the main race takes place. The event begins with the chief starter motioning the drivers to start their engines. After he is sure that all the drivers have started their engines, the chief starter raises the green flag, holds it up for a maximum of five seconds, and then drops it. The race is on, and it's every man for himself!

A rear view of the exciting start of an oval-track race

As mentioned earlier, the chief starter can disqualify a driver for reckless driving or for any other type of unsportsmanlike behavior, such as crowding or blocking. The chief starter can also stop a race if he thinks it necessary. When and if the race is restarted, all the drivers go back to the last officially counted lap. If only one lap has been raced, all the drivers return to their original starting positions. But if 60 percent or more of the laps have been completed when the race is stopped, the event is considered over. In this case, the winner is the driver who completed the most laps before the red flag was dropped.

In most oval-track races, all the laps are completed and the winner is the person who crosses the finish line first. If a driver is way out in the lead when his snowmobile suddenly conks out, he can still win the race by pulling or pushing his machine across the finish line. Even if he doesn't win, the driver will be counted as having completed the race if he manages to push *any part* of his machine over the finish line before the end of the race.

Three leading drivers fight it out for first place on the final lap of an oval-track race.

CROSS-COUNTRY RACING

A third type of snowmobile competition is cross-country racing. Like an oval-track race, a cross-country race is a test of speed. But with its rugged course laid out over lakes and islands, hills and valleys, woods and meadows, a cross-country race also tests a driver's skill and a machine's ability to withstand rough natural terrain.

Most cross-country courses are nine feet wide and between 20 and 50 miles long. In many cases, the courses pass through several different communities—one feature of cross-country racing that draws a lot of spectators and creates a lot of excitement. Since mandatory 10-minute rest stops for the drivers are usually located along the course, the snowmobile racers are given much needed breaks from the rugged conditions of cross-country racing. It's man against man in cross-country racing, with the snowmobile driver who covers the course in the least amount of time being the winner of the race.

Very long cross-country races—some up to 600 miles—are called "marathons." The Winnipeg to St. Paul 500-mile race and Alaska's Midnight Sun Race (600 miles from

The snowmobile drivers who participate in cross-country races must speed through woods, over hills, and across frozen lakes.

Anchorage to Fairbanks) are two of the longest and most famous snowmobile marathons. Since marathons are long, most of them are held over two or more days, with each driver being timed each day. Some marathons attract 100 or more drivers and many times as many spectators. Although snowmobile marathons are popular with drivers and spectators, they are becoming unpopular with sponsors. Sponsors have a hard time keeping track of all the drivers in a marathon, and they are not always able to discover accidents as quickly as they would like.

SLALOM RACING

Patterned after ski slaloms, slalom races for snowmobiles are downhill races held on zig-zag courses. An important feature of slalom racing is that the drivers race against the clock rather than against each other. One at a time, they guide their snowmobiles down the course, weaving in and out of a maze of right- and left-hand turns marked by flag-topped poles.

Slalom drivers are penalized one second for each pole they knock down and two seconds for each turn they miss. When the racers complete the course, the seconds they have accumulated as penalties are added to the time it took them to race from the starting line to the finish line. After all the drivers have completed the course, the one who has finished in the least amount of time is declared the winner.

Because of the penalties for hitting poles or for missing turns, skill is just as important in slalom racing as speed. In fact, slalom racing is so tricky that it is often called "obstacle racing." This explains why only the most experienced snowmobilers do well in slalom competition.

In a "snocross," a popular variation of a slalom race, snowmobilers race on a twisting, sloping course that includes several jumps.

HILLCLIMBING COMPETITION

Like slalom racing, hillclimbing is a difficult and demanding type of snowmobile competition. In hillclimbing events, snowmobile drivers attempt to race up and down a bumpy course laid out on a very steep hill or a mountainside. As in slalom racing, the drivers in hillclimbing events usually take on the course one at a time. Another similarity between slalom racing and hillclimbing is the emphasis on speed; in hillclimbing events, the driver who covers the course in the least amount of time is the winner.

Speed is important in hillclimbing competition, but then so is skill. Although a hill-climbing driver has no turns or poles to worry about, he must have excellent command of his machine in order to complete the course without toppling over. When climbing a steep hill, the driver must nurse the throttle of his machine and avoid accelerating too quickly. Coming down the hill can also be tricky. In order to reach the base of a hill without rolling over or running into a tree, a snowmobile driver must apply his brakes and go straight down the hill. If he goes down the hill too rapidly, or if he goes down at an angle, the driver runs the risk of losing control of his snowmobile and having it roll over sideways.

It takes much skill and experience for a snowmobile driver to successfully climb up a steep hill like this one.

DRAG RACING

Drag racing is becoming almost as popular with snowmobile drivers as it is with race-car drivers. As in automobile drag racing, the object of snowmobile drag racing is to zoom down a straight, smooth quarter-mile strip as quickly as possible. The main difference between drag racing for cars and drag racing for snowmobiles is in the drag strips: while cars usually drag race on paved straightaways, snowmobiles frequently drag race on frozen lakes.

When there are many entries in a snowmobile drag race, time trials are held to weed out the competing drivers. Each snowmobile must make at least one timed run down the drag strip, and only the drivers with the best times qualify for the "heats," which are the races that count. Two drivers race against each other in each heat, and the driver with the best time then competes against another driver in a second round of competition. This process of elimination continues until there is only one winner left. The winner of a snowmobile drag race is called the "top eliminator," just as he is in drag races for cars.

Because of its emphasis on speed, snowmobile drag racing is often called "sprint racing." In fact, the snowmobiles in drag racing competition reach such fantastic speeds that it is often impossible for a flagman or the spectators to tell who won. For this reason, many snowmobile drag strips have special timing systems at the finish line. These timing systems are so accurate that they can pick up split-second winning margins impossible to detect with the human eye.

A lightning-fast snowmobile covers a drag strip that has been laid out on a frozen lake.

CONCLUSION

Snowmobile racing is certainly one of the most exciting winter sports in the world. The cold air and white snow, the feel of the machine under you, the speed—all of these things combine to make for wonderful wintertime fun. (They also make for rosy cheeks and hearty appetites!)

Snowmobiling does, however, have one serious problem to deal with: as the sport is gaining more participants, it is becoming increasingly unpopular with the general public. Snowmobilers are being criticized for intruding upon private property, for hunting down deer and other wild animals, and for destroying the natural landscape with exhaust fumes and engine noise, with snowmobile tracks and litter. Although most snowmobilers are not guilty of these charges, a few thoughtless drivers are. Unfortunately, this minority has given snowmobiling a bad name and has branded *all* snowmobilers as "lawbreakers." As stricter laws and regulations are passed to control snowmobiling, it is hoped that the handful of lawless drivers will be weeded out and that honest snowmobilers will no longer be eyed with suspicion by the general public.

In spite of the black eye a few drivers have given the sport, snowmobiling—particularly snowmobile racing—is here to stay. As *the* winter sport, snowmobile racing is growing faster than any other type of motorized sport. Besides, as one 14-year-old boy put it, "It sure beats shoveling snow!"

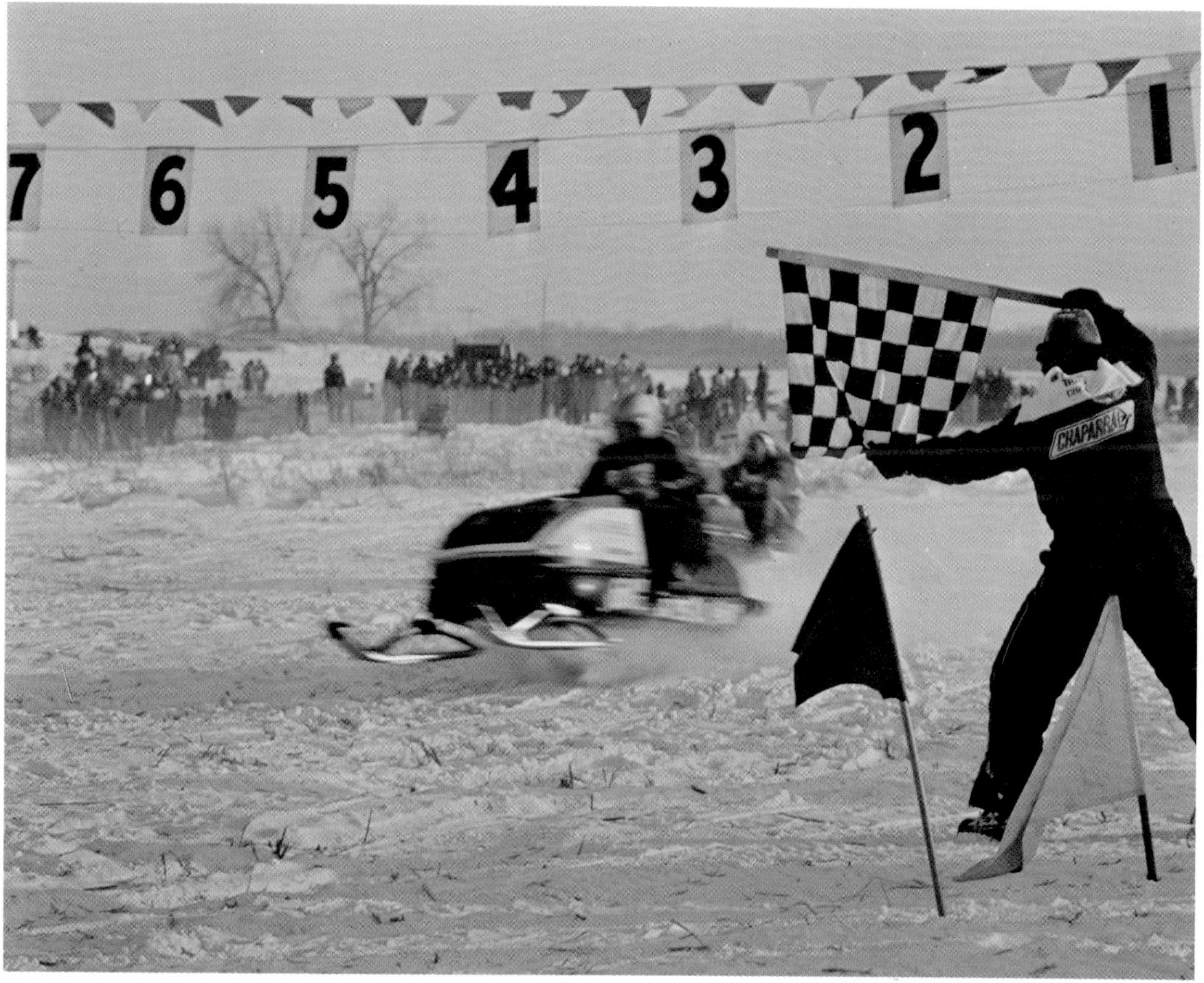
7
6
5
4
3
2
1
CHAPARRAL

Superwheels &
Thrill Sports

Lerner Publications Company
241 First Avenue North, Minneapolis, Minnesota 55401